THANKFUL IN ORDEALS

Thankful in Ordeals

by

H.G. Bishop Makary

Translated by

Yvonne Tadros

ST SHENOUDA MONASTERY
SYDNEY, AUSTRALIA
2015

THANKFUL IN ORDEALS

ST SHENOUDA MONASTERY
8419, Putty Rd,
Putty, NSW, 2330
Australia

www.stshenoudamonastery.org.au

ISBN 13: 978-0-9941910-2-1

Translated by:
Yvonne Tadros

Cover Design:
Hani Ghaly,
Begoury Graphics
begourygraphics@gmail.com

Contents

Preface

The Gospel tells us "Giving thanks always for all things to God the Father in the name of our Lord Jesus Christ" (Eph. 5:20). St. John Chrysostom tells us: "By a single word we regain all that we lost. Look at Job, his charity to the poor did not bear the same fruits as when he gave thanks during his afflictions." St. Gregory of Nazianzus says "...our being thankful is more essential than our breathing... There is time for everything, but being thankful is for all times". Origen says "He who thanks God in good times, is similar to someone who pays an owing debt; but he who gives thanks during hardships is similar to someone who gives God a loan!"

The late bishop Makary, Bishop of Sinai, in one of his golden sermons, teaches, "Being thankful during an ordeal helps bring the ordeal to an end". His golden sermons were evidence of his own life. His Grace lived a life of thanksgiving. He was constantly thankful because his lot in life was his Lord in that his whole life was a spent in praising God through thanksgiving for the way God treated both him and his congregation.

Thus, there is no place or time which does not

have the grace of God. No one that comes to Him leaves empty-handed. His mercies are renewed each morning. He who comes early to Him, finds Him. He who stays late at night, dines with Him. He always gives, there is no limit to His giving. All of us receive from Him, without limits. The late Abba Makary served Christ and his motto was, "Wherefore we receiving a kingdom which cannot be moved, let us have grace, whereby we may serve God acceptably with reverence and godly fear" (Heb. 12:28).

We thank God who blessed us to be contemporaries and witnesses of this true man of God, the late Abba Makary. He was a role model in everything especially since he preached what he did and did what he preached. Therefore, through his example, he presented a great harvest to the Lord Jesus.

We thank God who helped us in collating some of his golden sermons. We thank his loyal children in Christ who took this great task upon themselves. May the Lord reward all those who shared in this work. We ask this through the intercession of our Mother the Virgin Mary, the prayers of the Late Abba Makary, the prayers of H.H. Pope Shenouda III, and both his partners in the apostolic ministry: their Grace Abba Kozman (Bishop of Northern Sinai) and Abba Apollo (Bishop of Southern Sinai).

H.G. Abba Maximous,
Bishop of Banha and Quaisna
First day of Nineveh Fasting
17-2-2003

Introduction

I call upon each groaning soul burdened with affliction, whether it be illness, grief, or need. I call upon this soul to come and sit at the feet of the Lord Jesus, who dwells within Abba Makary. Tell him of the bitter sufferings and through the blessing of the Holy Spirit, who dwells within him and us, He will give us comfort and the balsamic healing for all these sufferings.

Through Abba Makary's sermon about "Being thankful in ordeals" he explains the subject with all its spiritual dimensions, the divine purpose for the test, how to handle it, how to pass through it safely, and how to obtain the blessings set aside in Heaven. The apostle St. Paul says: "For you have been privileged on behalf of Christ not only to believe in Him but also to suffer for Him" (Phi. 1:29). Thus, he demonstrates that pain or suffering is a "privilege" like the rest of the privileges the Lord Jesus blesses His chosen with.

A test or an ordeal for a non-believer translates into sadness, depression and hopelessness. However, for a believer, it means joy and glory; because it is a token of participation in the sufferings of The Lord in carrying the cross towards the ultimate aim of the Resurrection. Thus, if an ordeal is received with thanks and taken as a blessing from The Lord for one's own good and benefit, one will have a share in Heaven among the confessors and martyrs.

In this book, Abba Makary presents us with a lofty spiritual concept of the ordeal or test. Upon reading this book, the reader will realize that it is a guide to whoever is suffering and to whoever is walking in the way of our Lord Jesus Christ: the way of the Cross, the way of the saints and ultimately the way leading to the Kingdom of Heaven. Blessed is the soul who accepts the test with joy and thanks. They will be crowned and seated at the right of the throne of the Lord of Glory, our Lord Jesus Christ.

The book consists of sermons by the thrice beatified Abba Makary. May the Lord enlighten our hearts and minds to understand the treasures of blessing bestowed on us by accepting our tests and ordeals with endurance and thanks. We pray to our Lord Jesus Christ that this book be a source of blessing and salvation to many. We ask this through the intercession of our Lady the Mother of God, St. Mary, all the saints and through the prayers of H.H. Pope Shenouda III and his partners in the apostolic ministry, our fathers the Metropolitans and Bishops.

Glory be to our Lord for ever.
Abba Makary's Children in Christ

A Glimpse of Bishop Makary's Life

12.05.1940 - BORN

1961 - ATTAINED A BACHELOR OF ARCHITECTURE

25.08.1973 - ORDAINED A MONK IN ST. ABU MAQAR MONASTERY

1977 - SERVED IN EL-MENYA

1979 - SERVED IN ASSUIT

17.11.1988 - SERVED IN EL-AREISH

14.11.1996 - ORDAINED A BISHOP FOR THE SEE OF SINAI

25.07.2000 - REPOSED IN THE LORD

About the Author

Abba Makary was inclined towards quietness and tranquillity. Strangely he incorporated his quietness in his ministry. He worked quietly with no one knowing what he was doing until he actually completed the task and wherever he went he radiated peace, because he truly was a mobile monastery and a vessel of virtues. He prayed constantly. He believed that prayer sanctified all things and solved all problems regardless of their complexity. He did not allow his service to encroach on his prayer, as he considered prayer to be more important. He believed that it was through the power and grace of the Lord that we were able to serve.

His time was fully utilized in prayer, reading, church services, visiting the congregation, or being on work sites. He did not meet with people unless the meeting served a purpose. He did not like favouritism nor hypocrisy. He led a simple ascetic life in his manner of dress and in his food. He was frugal with whatever he was given. However, when it came to charity he did not lay down bounds nor limits. He gave generously without publicising.

The Lord blessed him with the grace of spiritual guidance with a standard equal to that of our forefathers. He built churches within his diocese and within monasteries and he upgraded many monasteries. In spite of the commitments to the numerous services within his diocese which demanded late nights and travelling, he was 'the simple cell-monk'. He was committed to all the monastic rules and vows in terms of prayers, praise and metanias.

He constantly quoted St. Pakhomious: "The saints were described as 'saints' because of their patience". He was a rock of endurance, patience and perseverance. He concealed his militancy, his suffering, his illness, and his problems. He carried his cross joyously, meeting everyone with a smile. Although the Lord blessed him with the ability to perform miracles, he also concealed this virtue.

A week before his departure, he visited one of the monasteries and bid them farewell saying that it was his last time to visit them. It was said that before his accident he had asked the chauffeur, "Are you prepared for the Kingdom now?" to which the chauffeur responded, "No, I have children". He then replied, "Then, I shall go and leave you for your children". And so it was.

Chapter 1

The necessity of thanking God constantly

A spiritual person is equally thankful for an ordeal as well as for a blessing, because the ordeal is a blessing

- Pope Shenouda III

The Church taught us to begin each prayer with the Thanksgiving Prayer where we say "We thank You for every condition, in any condition, and in all conditions". When righteous Job blessed God, he said "May the Lord's Name be blessed". Blessing God means praising and thanking Him for everything. St. Isaac the Syrian says: "There is no talent without increase, except the one which is not accompanied by thanks".

Being thankful in the face of ordeals helps bring the ordeal to an end. Being thankful is an indication of God's forthcoming blessings. Whining, which is the opposite of thanking, does not help in the event of affliction, ordeals, or in the chastening of a person. A unnamed saint says: "Through affliction, ordeals, or illness, thank God. Do not grumble and know that all is for your own good. If it is God's will to lift it, he would have done so. But He does not, because in a test He sees your good and your salvation, and when God's purpose is realized the ordeal is lifted".

In our prayers we focus mainly on our needs, we ask for a great deal. Regrettably, most of us overlook thanking our Lord. This is especially so in the event of an affliction, test, pain, need, illness, or persecution. Being thankful is the evidence of a 'live faith'. The greatest thanking is one given when facing a test or ordeal. When one is happy, successful and not in need and gives thanks, one ought to do so. It means that one does not forget the Lord's blessings. But this is not the same as a person who is thankful during pain, ordeal, test, need, persecution, and/or deprivation.

The following story demonstrates about endurance

and being thankful. A very poor man once asked St. Makarious of Alexandria to allow him to reside in a cell near him in order to share in his prayers. St. Makarious said : "This will be a blessing for me". The poor man built a cell near St. Abu Maqar of Alexandria and lived in it. St. Abu Maqar of Alexandria was a hermit by nature and did not socialize much. He noticed that that man was extremely poor and greatly ascetic.

On a very cold winter night, Abu Maqar felt the bite of the cold, as the raindrops were icy and it was a star-less and dark night. He walked with difficulty until he reached his friend's cell. He saw that he was still awake and heard him talking to God: "Thank you Lord, for there are many wars whereby kings are conquered by their enemies, stripped of their possessions, tortured, and deprived of their families, but I did not lose anything. Thank you Lord, for there are many people who, because of the intensity of their illness, cannot even move from bed, but here I am moving freely with both healthy arms and legs. Thank you Lord for there are many who are now in prisons, in fetters, being tortured and are having limbs amputated, and here I am with healthy limbs. Thank you so much O Lord, I praise You for blessing me with good health, sound mind, free will and making me physically fit in all aspects."

St. Abu Maqar was greatly touched when he listened to the thankful prayer and praise of this poor man in spite of all what he was going through. He was under rain and snow, with nothing to warm him, but nevertheless, he happily praised the Lord with all his heart. While Abu Maqar was watching this poor man's cell, he noticed that it was divinely lit, with the poor man within. Thus, our saintly forefathers say: "A person who does not thank God when one has only little, this person is not genuine when they thank God only when they have plenty".

Chapter 2

The Lord urges His disciples to go through the test

"If you think that you can walk in the way of the Lord without any tests, then know that you are walking outside and far from it; you are not following the footsteps of the saints"

- St. Isaac the Syrian.

"Immediately Jesus made His disciples get into the
boat and go on ahead of Him to Bethsaida, while He
dismissed the crowd. After leaving them, He went up
on a mountainside to pray. Later that night, the boat
was in the middle of the lake, and He was alone on land.
He saw the disciples straining at the oars, because the
wind was against them. Shortly before dawn he went
out to them, walking on the lake. He was about to pass
by them, but when they saw Him walking on the lake,
they thought He was a ghost. They cried out, because
they all saw Him and were terrified. Immediately He
spoke to them and said, "Take courage! It is I. Don't be
afraid." Then He climbed into the boat with them, and
the wind died down. They were completely amazed,
for they had not understood about the loaves; their
hearts were hardened. (Mk.6:45-53)

THE ORDEALS STRENGTHEN THE FAITH

"Immediately Jesus made His disciples get into the
boat and go on ahead of Him". He ordered them to
cross over to the other side. During their crossing, they
faced hardships and ordeals: they faced drowning
and death. However, undergoing these tests was
demanded by the Lord Jesus, because crossing over
was not the disciples' choice but the Lord's.

Why did the Lord demand that His disciples
undergo this test ? Because The Lord Jesus already
knew that their faith was weak. He wanted to elevate
them to a higher level of faith. This could not be realized
unless they faced a test. For example, a person may
experience a situation where they say to themselves: I
wish I did not take this trip; or I wish I did not listen to

so and so. All this would not have happened. To this person I say: All this would not have changed God's intention in His purpose towards you. Because His purpose was that it was necessary for you to undergo this test. Because only through this test will you know your weakness and lack of faith. Through the test, Jesus reveals to you His power and authority when He comes to you, steps on the waves, silences the tempest and turns the darkness into light.

Our faith in God becomes stronger according to the severity of the ordeal. "My brothers, consider it a great joy when trials of many kinds come upon you, for you well know that the testing of your faith produces perseverance, and perseverance must complete its work so that you will become fully developed, complete, not deficient in any way." (James 1:2-4) Thus, it is through the tests which God commits us to undergo, that we become "fully developed and complete". In other words, if we thankfully endure ordeals, we grow spiritually to reach perfection.

"But when they saw Him walking on the lake, they thought He was a ghost. They cried out, because they all saw Him and were terrified." Can anyone who sees Jesus be terrified? Yes, because the despair resulting from the severity of an ordeal, allows one to see reality as surreal and even when the Lord Jesus is close to a person during ordeals, one remains fearful and agitated. Due to the severity of an ordeal, a person may lose all hope and become totally desperate, in which case one may lose the sense of being close to God. He becomes entirely dominated by darkness, amidst the suffering he cannot see an outlet, nor a beam of light at the end of the tunnel.

The Lord patiently waits in order to save us because a person rejoices at the end of an ordeal because as much as his suffering and endurance were, his faith in God will have grown. The second reason is that in the dark hours which a person goes through during an ordeal, brightens the Lord's light on His arrival to silence the tempestuous sea; that is, the darker the hours are, the brighter is God's light. If the ordeal and the suffering are long, then we say to ourselves "dawn will arrive soon. The Lord will answer my prayers, even if He takes His time and even if I stay amidst the darkness, The Lord is my Light"

"Be aware that the closer you are to the Kingdom and God's city, the more you will be faced with tests whose intensity will increase in proportion to your growth and progress." - St. Isaac the Syrian

PRAYERS DURING ORDEALS

"Prayers before an ordeal are similar to a prayer of someone who is alien to God. However, prayer during an ordeal is counted by God as a prayer of a loving faithful. It is like making God indebted to you." - St. Isaac the Syrian.

But when they saw Him walking on the lake, they thought He was a ghost. They cried out, because they all saw Him and were terrified. Actually as a result of the fear of darkness, fear and anxiety dominate thoughts and feelings. What was the use of their crying? Their crying led Jesus to answer them "It is I. Do not be afraid."

What is the meaning of crying during an ordeal? It means earnest prayer. The greatest prayer is the one said in the middle of a hardship, similar to Jonah's prayer from within the whale when he was surrounded by water, the secretions of the whale's stomach and all the weeds. He could hardly breathe for the lack of oxygen. He felt that he was inside a tomb for three days. He lost hope of survival but he said "… from the depth of the abyss, I cried to the Lord". One who does not cry during an ordeal, will not hear the Lord's voice saying, "It is I. Do not be afraid."

One may say: I am so ill and suffering so much, I cannot stand up for prayer. I say, pray and cry to the Lord while you are seated. One may say: I am no longer able to pray the same way I used to, neither time nor quality-wise. My answer is: Our Lord does not ask you for how much or in what manner you pray, because according to St. Isaac the Syrian, "prayer is the mind's cry of a broken heart". During an ordeal, a prayer is more fervent and more sincere especially when it is from the depth of darkness and during the suffering of the ordeal. God is quick to answer who cries to Him during an ordeal … "and call upon Me in the day of trouble; I will deliver you, and you shall glorify Me." (Ps.50:15)

After calling Peter to walk to Him, as he was walking on water and shortly before reaching Jesus, Peter was afraid: "But when he saw the wind, he was afraid and, beginning to sink, cried out, "Lord, save me!" (Matt. 14:30)

"Lord, save me". A prayer of three words and not three hours. But how did he say it? He said it sincerely, earnestly, genuinely, and with all his heart and soul. Regrettably, some people pray like parrots, and recite psalms without understanding what they say. Prayer must come from the heart. One must understand what they say and must be sincere. "The person who wishes to overcome tests without prayers, falls deeper into the tests" St. Mark.

When Jesus told His disciples to take courage and not to fear, it meant that His answer and reassurance were immediate. His presence among us is constant to the end of times. "And behold, I am with you always, to the end of the age." (Matt. 28:20). It also meant that Jesus has not changed. True, our feelings towards Him change, because sometimes we feel as if He is far from us, and sometimes we feel He is close, even though He is everywhere and among us all the time. In the Mass there is a prayer called "The Pauline Incense Prayer" which is said by the priest silently at the altar before the Pauline Reading: "O Great Eternal God, You have no beginning and have no end, You are great in wisdom, mighty in Your acts, You are everywhere and within everyone, be with us now".

"Then He climbed into the boat with them, and the wind died down" Did that mean that before then, Jesus was not present in the boat? Actually, the Lord was and is present all the time and everywhere. However, the disciples did not feel His presence. Thus, in an ordeal a person loses the feeling of God's presence, even though He is close to that person during ordeals and in all life situations.

"...and the wind died down". According to the spiritual concept, the wind is a symbol of evil i.e.

Satan. There is a common Arabic saying: "Shut the door which lets in the wind and you will be in peace". This means that when Satan fights you, he knows your weak point and takes advantage of it. In order to have peace, shut that door! Satan also knows what irritates or provokes a person. Let us say, he knows that a person is annoyed by a loud voice. He goes and makes his wife nag him day and night in a loud voice. In order not to give Satan a chance, the husband shuts this door by being patient, because love endures all things. There are many ways and means whereby Satan is capable of making us deviate from God's way. It is for us to be vigilant through prayer and to thus shut all doors in his face.

BEFORE THE ORDEAL, GOD GRANTS THE BLESSING

Before God allows a person to be the subject of a test, He gives that person additional blessings such as the ability to endure and pass through that ordeal. This was what took place with the disciples before the Lord Jesus subjected them to the boat test. He revealed to them His authority through the miracle of the five loaves. It was through seeing His power, that they believed in Him and went down to the sea, where they were tested. However, even after the miracle, the disciples failed to understand, "And He got into the boat with them, and the wind ceased. And they were utterly astounded, for they did not understand about the loaves, but their hearts were hardened" (Mk.6:51-52)

The disciples themselves collected the food left over after the Lord blessed the loaves and fish. They were wondering at His authority over the material creation and were blessed with the grace of faith. They saw His authority over the power of nature (the tempest), yet their faith weakened when it came to the rescue of the boat. It begs the question, didn't they realize that He watched them and their boat? Before the test, the disciples were blessed with firm faith in the Lord, after which they were immediately tested.

"But with the temptation he will also provide the way of escape, that you may be able to endure it."(1 Cor. 10:13) What is the way of escape? It is that He will:
. Give you the blessing of a means of support to help endure the test, or
. Give you enough faith, or
. Give you inner peace, or
. Send His Spirit to comfort you, or
. Send His angel to guide you to endure

We find that some people are blessed with inner peace, in spite of the harshness of their test. Some liken themselves to the three lads who were in the furnace and felt that they had a fourth companion.....they say "we feel God's presence with us". Also, the priest concludes the prayer for the sick by saying: "Lord grant mercy, give comfort, give blessing, give help, give salvation, grant forgiveness of sins, refresh all the souls who are suffering and who are in any form of grip"

There was an incident which was mentioned only by St. Matthew: "And Peter answered Him and said, Lord, if it be thou, bid me come unto Thee on the water."(Matt. 14:28) It was through faith that Peter realized that if it were the Lord's will that he should walk on water, he could. Consequently, a person could be given this power through grace and this is a theological fact i.e. all that Jesus had performed during His incarnation on this earth, will be bestowed upon the believers through the Holy Spirit.

Focus on The Lord and you will be saved from the test

In St. Peter's example, it is noticed that when he walked on the water he started to fall only when his attention was distracted towards the strength of the wind i.e. he lost his focus on the Lord. Similarly, when we are subjected to a test, the moment we focus on the surrounding circumstances, we lose our focus on Jesus and become subject to our weaknesses. Why pay attention to Satan, thinking that he is stronger than you? It is true, he is stronger than you, me, or anyone else, but Jesus is mightier than every power. He is our armor and shield. Do not fear the wind, do not listen to Satan's voice who leads you to doubt. The wind may be mighty, the sea may be tempestuous, the ordeal may be hard to bear, but once the Lord steps on the waves, He restores the calm. He shines with His light in the darkness "even the darkness will not be dark to you; the night will shine like the day, for darkness is as light to You." (Ps.139:12)

Harsh ordeals are for the steadfast in faith

When God tests a person, the test is according to one's endurance. We always argue that we are tested beyond our endurance. However, God never allows a person to suffer beyond their own endurance (1 Cor. 1:13). The extent of the saints' firmness in faith is measured by the extent of their suffering "your success in spirituality is gauged by the severity of your ordeals. The more the ordeals, the more the grace" - St. Maximous

Harsh ordeals are sent to strong people with great faith. The people who shared in the miracle of the five loaves did not enter the boat, that is, they were not chosen for the test. Those who entered were the disciples, because hard tests are not sent to average believers. What do we mean by average people? They are the ones who know that our Lord is sweet because He gives them their needs: money, food, clothing, good positions and they thank God for all these but that's the end of their relationship with Him.

The Lord asks those who are deep in their faith to accept the ordeals, while facing the depths of the sea and tempests. The concept of ordeals by the true believer is different to the concept for the average person. The true believer's thinking is, "God loves me. That's why He is testing me and that's why I am thankful that He is testing me. Also, the Lord disciplines the one He loves, and He chastens everyone He accepts as His." (Heb. 12:6)

Often, a person's ordeal is not limited merely to one's suffering, but becomes intensified by the scorn of others, especially when told by others (through Satan's insinuation) that his devotion is all fake and his suffering is a result of his sin and hypocrisy. While, on the contrary, the ordeal is a form of blessing bestowed by God on His own. "The greatness of the blessing is according to the immensity of the ordeal. This is how God grades the blessing. The greater the test, the greater is the blessing" - St. Isaac the Syrian

THE ORDEAL IS THE SUSTENANCE OF THE SOUL

Food is a means to sustains the body and ordeals is a means to sustain the soul. It was said that a monk passed through an extremely long and painful illness. Later on, he had a healthy, peaceful and pain-free year. He was not subjected to the usual pain which he suffered each year. This saint prayed asking the Lord, "Lord, are You displeased with me? Why did You not send me the sustenance which You give me each year? Have I sinned against You? "This saint knew the merits of ordeals for spiritual growth and the ultimate joy earned for heavenly glory.

Ordeals indicate that we are walking on the correct path: on the 'way of the Cross' leading to the Kingdom. "If you were of the world, the world would love you as its own; but because you are not of the world, but I chose you out of the world, therefore the world hates you." (Jn. 15:19)

"When you see a sick person say: blessed is the person whom God made worthy to be tested in the ways of inheriting [eternal] life" - St. Isaac the Syrian

Chapter 3

There is no salvation, except through Christ

"Ordeals are as close to people as eyelids are to the eyes. In His wisdom, God planned it that way so that you constantly knock on His door out of concern about ordeals. Thus, your heart becomes sanctified through constantly calling upon His Name"

- St. Isaac the Syrian.

A CONTEMPORARY STORY ABOUT BEING THANKFUL IN OR-
DEALS

This story is about a man who worked as a
contractor. He was very smart and very successful in
his work; he was healthy and of solid build. He was
so smart that he used to take more than one job at the
same time, and he organized his work both in terms
of time and sequentially. In other words, an existing
job depended on the completion of the previous one
in terms of finances. He would say to himself "this job
will be completed after two months" and he would
then take another job. He would think to himself that
by the time he received the money from the two jobs,
he could start another two new jobs, and so on. Thus,
he engaged in several jobs on different sites.

As he narrowed the time gaps between jobs, the
completion of the work in time became unsustainable.
One day, which he started full of optimism and in
anticipation of success, on that very same day, he
ended up with utter failure, and after being a multi-
millionaire, ended up accumulating debts of250,000
pounds. How did this happen? The labourers were
working on a job when the liquid cash on that day
was short. It is a known fact, that contractors carry out
their work through bank loans; also they have credits
with government and other organizations for whom
they are contracted for work.

On that day, the labourers on that particular site
did not receive their wages. When they went to the
foreman to ask for their wages, he told them to wait
for the contractor. The labourers refused to wait. They
rebelled, took the contractor's work tools without

completing the work and quit. When a second group in another site heard of what had happened, they did the same. Not only that, they contacted a third group. Within a few hours, this was repeated at several sites. At the end of the day, they all quit work, taking with them the contractor's man-power and their tools.

Unfortunately, within a few hours the news reached the sub-contractors who carried minor jobs for him. Hearing that the labourers did not receive their wages, they left the work sites, telephoned him and asked for immediate payment of their entitlements. The contractor asked them to give him time until he received part-payment of the sums due to him from the contracting authorities, because he did not have enough cash for immediate payments. Also the work for which he was supposed to receive these payments was not completed as of yet. They refused his offer and left the sites. No doubt, Satan was behind all this. He incited the workers and sub-contractors to leave their work-sites, leading to the work being incomplete and ending up with the Contractor's bankruptcy.

Shortly after, the news reached the banks who contacted him asking him for repayment of his debts, threatening no further dealings with him. This wasn't the worst of it. On the same day, he received notification from the Government that he owed 100,000 pounds in taxes and insurance fees. It was not known how the Government came to know and whether this was through the banks or through his employees. He was asked for immediate repayment; otherwise he would be deregistered as a contractor. He asked them to give him time until he collected money that was owed to him, but the Government refused. They immediately seized all his assets, and removed his name from the Contractors' Register. He was not allowed to work as a contractor unless he settled all his debts.

His lawyer advised him to declare bankruptcy. However, being a determined and ambitious person, he declined this suggestion. He sold his home and other properties and lived in a leased home. He was successful and determined, and although what happened to him took place in a single day, he was still proud of himself. He thought to himself "I am still healthy and my family are all well" .The following day he received a call from his daughter's school notifying him that his daughter was taken to hospital; suspected of suffering meningitis. He and his wife went to the hospital. On the way he was praying: "Please God, let it be something else, other than meningitis". Through God's compassion, the final diagnosis eliminated meningitis.

Following this incident, his wife could not endure any more hardships; and so she was on the verge of a break-down. Eventually, the contractor's health began to fail. He could no longer be of any help to others or himself. There was no longer any time for God in his life and even though he was a church member, it was more in an honorary nature or as a social gathering. He rarely attended church.

One day the contractor lay on his back and as he gazed at the ceiling of his bedroom, he reflected for the first time on what had happened to him. He was trying to grasp the past events which led to that tragic end, despite the fact he was an honest and successful man. He could not help his tears. At this moment he could hear the voice of the Divine Father saying: "I want you to dedicate your life to serving Me". The Contractor said: "There is nothing left in my life to offer You. However, if You help me to stand on my feet once again, I will offer You my life." In his prayer, the Contractor also asked God to make something in his life worth living for.

Shortly after, he heard that a gifted preacher would be at church speaking to businessmen about God's Word. He felt a desire to attend and to listen to this sermon. The preacher spoke about being unconditionally thankful, especially during catastrophes, hardships, illnesses and ordeals. Being thankful in ordeals moves God either to put an end to the ordeal or to give the person the blessing so as to be above the ordeal.

This sermon about being thankful moved him. He had a deep feeling which he never experienced before: hope and faith in God. He thought to himself: "If this preacher is right, it means I still have a chance to thank God for what I have been through. There must be a purpose which I cannot fathom for all that has happened to me". He realized that God brought him to that moment only because He had intended that he carry out a special mission for Him.

Several months later, he heard that the same preacher was delivering a sermon in a nearby town's church. He thought to himself "I'll go. The venue is close, and I have nothing to do". He attended the sermon, and sat with the preacher and told him of all that had happened to him. The preacher comforted him and spoke of the merits of being thankful. The contractor felt that a great burden was lifted off his shoulders. Eventually, the contractor decided to move close to the Church to which the preacher was attached.

It happened at that time that the townsfolk were thinking of building a new church. The preacher asked the contractor, being a successful and experienced person in that area, to take a look at the plans of the proposed church. He asked the Contractor, after perusing the plans, to present them to the Council for approval to proceed with the building.

The Contractor took home a copy of the plans, and after perusal he found out that they were totally unsuitable. He told his friend that the plans were technically faulty, and that they were intended for an architecturally old, classic building, that they very costly and needed special artisans, and that the area allowed very limited accommodation (400 people) without any possibility for future extensions. In other words it was not practical in many aspects. The plans were given to the Contractor for re-drafting and to eventually carry out the project. He redesigned the plans to accommodate 800 persons, with the possibility of future extensions to accommodate 1200 persons, all at the same cost. The contractor then remained without work for 18 months, thanking the Lord all the time.

Sometime later, a Government representative paid him a visit to get information about how he was managing his situation. The representative told him that he would submit a report based on the information provided, with the hope that things might improve. Two months later, the representative called him telling him that the government looked into his case and confirmed that it was not possible for the contractor to repay his debts since he was not permitted to continue working. Therefore, the government approved a loan of 5000 and granted him permission to resume work.

The contractor was asked to build a house for someone. This was followed by a sequence of requests for building projects, which, in time, allowed him to repay all his debts and be financially stable. The experience made a new person of the contractor. He became a true believer in God. All his conversations focused on our Lord, and his money was dedicated to serving our Lord. He understood God's purpose in subjecting him to the test.

This is a true and contemporary example of a man, who was subjected to a hard ordeal, who then thanked our Lord, leading to help for him to overcome it, in due time. "No one enters the Kingdom unless they are tested first" - St. Anthony

"The spiritual interpretation for the word "ordeals" is "blessings and crowns". This is the spiritual language, and if you try to interpret it otherwise, you will face problems" - Pope Shenouda III.

Chapter 4

Bethesda's Invalid Man: A model of patience and perseverance in ordeals

"If God wishes to relieve His true children, He does not take away their ordeals but gives them the strength to endure them."

- St. Isaac the Syrian

"After this there was a feast of the Jews, and Jesus went up to Jerusalem. Now there is at Jerusalem by the sheep market a pool, which is called in the Hebrew tongue Bethesda, having five porches. In these lay a great multitude of sick folk, blind, halt, withered, waiting for the moving of the water. For an angel went down at a certain season into the pool, and troubled the water: whosoever then first after the troubling of the water stepped in was made whole of whatsoever disease he had. And a certain man was there, which had an infirmity thirty and eight years. When Jesus saw him lying there , and knew that he had been now a long time in that case, he saith unto him, Wilt thou be made whole? The sick man answered him, Sir, I have no man, when the water is troubled, to put me into the pool: but while I am coming, another steppeth down before me. Jesus saith unto him, Rise, take up thy bed, and walk. And immediately the man was made whole, and took up his bed, and walked: and on the same day was the Sabbath. (Jn. 5:1-9)

I AWAITED THE LORD, I AWAITED THE LORD

In these lay a great multitude of sick folk waiting for the moving of the water. The angel went down at a certain season and stirred the water. The invalid people watched and waited for the moment of the stirring of the water. The spiritual concept here is that the spiritually sick should constantly be waiting and be ready for the visit of Grace - " I'm ready, God, so ready (Ps. 57:7)."

When a sick person ignores this grace, or is detached from it, this person will definitely not be healed. For this reason, Jesus tells us to always be alert and prepared "Watch therefore, for ye know neither the day nor the hour wherein the Son of man cometh." (Mt. 25:13) We do not know whether by coming, Jesus means His coming for Judgment Day, or for the time of our departure, or in His visits to attend to us. The same applies when Jesus knocks on our door. If we do not open because we are preoccupied with other issues, we will not gain any reward. "Here I am! I stand at the door and knock. If anyone hears my voice and opens the door, I will come in and eat with that person, and they with me."(Rev. 3:20)

And a certain man was there, which had an infirmity thirty and eight years. The Bethesda invalid man was a quadriplegic, totally immobile. In other words, if he wanted to turn on his side or if he needed to go to the bathroom, someone had to help him. No doubt he felt great bitterness, he was broken, and humiliated with nothing to look forward to amidst his miserable life. For 38 years he laid down there waiting near the lake enduring the scorching sun and the freezing cold. When Jesus saw him lying there, He knew that he had been there a long time.

True, there were many sick people around the lake, but the Lord Jesus saw this man as being different to all the others. He knew that his need for healing was greater than that of any of them. This person reached the edge of despair, because had he actually been desperate, he would have left the lakeside ages before. He would have thought to himself: "I am unlucky, I know if I stay for 50 years beside this lake I will not be healed; this is my fate. It seems God has His favourites, He loves all people but I am not one of them". However, he did not react that way. He was patient and endured his sufferings.

Sometimes we are impatient even with small tests and whine asking the Lord as to why we are subjected to the test, while Bethesda's invalid suffered for 38 years, not 38 months, weeks or days. He witnessed daily cases of various healing which he narrowly missed, and even though his ordeal totally crushed him, he never despaired.

God did not forget nor did He ignore him. He allowed the ordeal to continue for 38 years to give us and the whole human race an example of patience and perseverance. God wanted us to reflect on the extent of that man's suffering: how much he endured: his bad odour, his depression, and his loneliness for 38 years without friends, relatives - absolutely no one. Jesus had pity on him thinking "Enough. Suffices him what he had been through. With these sufferings, I have perfected him". "Son though He was, He learned obedience from what He suffered and, once made perfect, He became the source of eternal salvation for all who obey Him"(Heb. 5:8-9)

Obviously, the Bethesda invalid faced wars waged by Satan telling him "Where is your Lord whom you worship? Why didn't He heal you? Why didn't He send you someone to drop you in the lake? Is your sin greater than that of others? All those who were around you were healed and you are still sick. Where is your God?" One may often feel resentment saying: "I prayed and God did not answer my prayer. Why has He not answered me until now? " St. Peter clarifies this, "The Lord is not slow in keeping His promise, as some understand slowness. Instead He is patient with you, not wanting anyone to perish, but everyone to come to repentance." (2Pet.3:9)

INEVITABILITY OF PAIN TO ATTAIN GLORY

Pain and ordeals are inevitable. St. Paula says "He who evades an ordeal, evades God". St. Paul the Apostle says: "And if children, then heirs — heirs of God and fellow heirs with Christ, provided we suffer with Him in order that we may also be glorified with Him."(Rom.8:17).

Do not think that when a person's life is comfortably smooth one feels happy about it. When we encounter hardships or persecution we should not wonder. On the contrary, we should wonder if our life on earth goes smoothly without any hardships or disappointments. If you are to be a saint, your life must have tests, pain and a cross to bear. "Do not be surprised at the fiery ordeal that has come on you to test you, as though something strange were happening to you". (1 Pet. 4:12) "In fact, everyone who wants to live a godly life in Christ Jesus will be persecuted." (2Tim.3:12)

"We must go through many hardships to enter the kingdom of God". (Acts 14:22) The presence of hardships in one's life indicates one's step towards the narrow path leading to eternal life in the Kingdom. Why lose peace when you fall sick? Rejoice and think to yourself that you have walked the greater part of the way and you are approaching its end. "Rejoice in that day and leap for joy ..... " (Lk. 6:23)

It is a worry if a person's life is hardship-free. It is similar to a person who sets on a journey without provision for sustenance, or someone who does not deposit money ahead of a journey in order to find it upon arrival. "Be concerned if your path is peaceful all the way. This means that you are far from the correct path trodden by the saints." - St. Maximous

GRACE SUSTAINS THE TEMPTED IN A MYSTERIOUS WAY

"When Jesus saw him lying there , and knew that he had been now a long time in that case, He saith unto him, Wilt thou be made whole?"

When Jesus asked this question, He did not mean it in the sense whether the man wished to be healed or not, the intention was to express extreme compassion and pity. It was with great love He asked the question as if to say "Do you wish to feel better?" In other words: 'I know that you want to be healed and I came especially for you. "Are not two sparrows sold for a penny? Yet not one of them will fall to the ground outside your Father's care." (Mt. 10:29) Never think that I forgot you, now is the time for your healing. If it seems to you that I ignored you, I never did and never will. I am watching over you throughout your life'.

My grace strengthened and supported you; each day I gave you strength to endure. You were an example to the people, similar to John the Baptist: not swayed by the wind: "What did you go out into the wilderness to see? A reed swayed by the wind?" (Mt. 11:7)

In fact, there are some who are swayed by the wind who is Satan. One day they are swayed towards a certain direction, the next they are swayed towards another, but the sick man of Bethesda was like a house built on the rock, and not that built on sand. Also, Jesus' question inferred that a person, in order to be healed, must have the will to repent, because sin is a source of illness. Healing is not one-sided, you also must take part and your part is to repent and pray to God seeking healing.

This is further demonstrated in Jesus' words "Jerusalem, Jerusalem, you who kill the prophets and stone those sent to you, how often I have longed to gather your children together, as a hen gathers her chicks under her wings, and you were not willing. Look, your house is left to you desolate. I tell you, you will not see me again until you say, 'Blessed is he who comes in the name of the Lord'."(Lk. 13: 34-35)

ORDEALS SHOW FAITH

"Sir, I have no man, when the water is troubled, to put me into the pool: but while I am coming, another steppeth down before me."

Here, the sick man, in his mind, tells the Lord: "The obstacle to my healing is beyond my will. It is not due to a fault on my part or because of a lack of my faith. I did not miss a day in being next to the lake; I did not lose my faith, not for a second, and despite all these sufferings and all the wars waged by Satan against me, I am still clinging to the Lord and with hope waiting for Him." The Psalmist says: "Wait for the LORD; be strong and take heart and wait for the

Lord" - Psalm 27:14 and now, it is time that Psalm 40:1 is applicable to me, "I waited patiently for the Lord; He turned to me and heard my cry." "Never did I hold a grudge against those who ran to the lake before me. Never did I question God's will in healing them and not me. I knew God had a purpose which is always for our good. I never judged any of those who were healed before me. True, I suffered emotionally after they were healed, because they all deserted me after they were healed. None of them thought of returning to help me being dropped into the lake or even visit me. On the contrary, I prayed that God may forgive them."

"Jesus saith unto him, Rise, take up thy bed, and walk." The invalid was in a state of awe. He must have thought to himself : "I rise, take up my bed!! All I was asking was to walk, even one step; as for the bed, I would have asked someone to carry it for me." But the Lord's gift was the ultimate of perfection: complete healing and full strength - all within a second. "Without ordeals you are unable to feel God's compassion, you are unable to fathom the purpose of the Spirit and you are unable to sense the Divine Yearning." - St. Isaac

GIVING THANKS AT THE END OF AN ORDEAL

"Jesus saw him in the Temple"
Following his healing, the Temple was the first place the invalid visited in order to give thanks to our Lord for the miracle. Regrettably, there are some who remember our Lord only during ordeals or problems. Once these are over, they forget to thank our Lord, which was not the case with Bethesda's invalid.

"Sorrows sent to us are only an evidence of God's care for us." - St. Isaac the Syrian

Chapter 5

Job: A Role Model of being thankful in ordeals

We have Job as a role model for all generations: "Behold, we consider those blessed who remained steadfast. You have heard of the steadfastness of Job, and you have seen the purpose of the Lord."

- James 5:11

"The Lord said to Satan, "Where have you come from?" Satan answered the Lord, "From roaming throughout the earth, going back and forth on it." Then the Lord said to Satan, "Have you considered my servant Job? There is no one on earth like him; he is blameless and upright, a man who fears God and shuns evil." "Does Job fear God for nothing?" Satan replied. "Have You not put a hedge around him and his household and everything he has? You have blessed the work of his hands, so that his flocks and herds are spread throughout the land. But now stretch out Your hand and strike everything he has, and he will surely curse You to Your face." The Lord said to Satan, "Very well, then, everything he has is in your power, but on the man himself do not lay a finger."

Then Satan went out from the presence of the Lord. One day when Job's sons and daughters were feasting and drinking wine at the oldest brother's house, a messenger came to Job and said, "The oxen were plowing and the donkeys were grazing nearby, and the Sabeans attacked and made off with them. They put the servants to the sword, and I am the only one who has escaped to tell you!"

While he was still speaking, another messenger came and said, "The fire of God fell from the heavens and burned up the sheep and the servants, and I am the only one who has escaped to tell you!" While he was still speaking, another messenger came and said, "The Chaldeans formed three raiding parties and swept down on your camels and made off with them. They put the servants to the sword, and I am the only one who has escaped to tell you!"

While he was still speaking, yet another messenger came and said, "Your sons and daughters were feasting and drinking wine at the oldest brother's house, when suddenly a mighty wind swept in from the desert and struck the four corners of the house. It collapsed on them and they are dead, and I am the only one who has escaped to tell you!" At this, Job got up and tore his robe and shaved his head. Then he fell to the ground in worship and said: "Naked I came from my mother's womb, and naked I will depart. The Lord gave and the Lord has taken away; may the name of the Lord be praised." In all this, Job did not sin by charging God with wrongdoing. (Job 1:7-22)

The Lord said to Satan, "Where have you come from?" Satan answered the Lord, "From roaming throughout the earth, going back and forth on it." The Lord knows what goes in people's minds. He knows who Satan plots against, which reminds us of what St. Peter preached: " Be sober, be vigilant; because your adversary the devil walks about like a roaring lion, seeking whom he may devour. Resist him, steadfast in the faith." (1 Pet. 5:8-9).

When Satan said that he was roaming throughout the earth, this meant that he was actively working. Therefore, a person must be vigilant towards Satan's temptations. Let us listen carefully to what Satan said about Job: "Have You not put a hedge around him and his household and everything he has?" This means that he was helpless against God's protection because "The angel of the LORD encamps around those who fear him, and he delivers them." (Ps.34:7) and the angel of the LORD encamped around Job and all his household and his properties; and thus he was untouchable by any evil power. Satan's argument was that Job's righteousness was hypocritical and only because the LORD bountifully blessed him in all aspects. Once these blessings were taken away from him, his false piety would go and he would blaspheme.

SATAN ASKS TO BE ALLOWED TO TEST JOB

This means that Satan does not have the freedom to test God's children unless God allows him to do so, and even then, it is within limits, and at a time determined by God.

The First Test

A messenger came to Job and said, "The oxen were plowing and the donkeys were grazing nearby, and the Sabeans attacked and made off with them. They put the servants to the sword, and I am the only one who escaped to tell you ....." The Sabeans had been Job's neighbours for years. Why did they attack at this particular time ? Evidently, with God's permission, Satan incited evil in the people (the Sabeans) who "made off" with the cattle and killed the servants.

As for me, if people are unfair to me, or persecute or hurt me in any way, I do not blame them, because they do not behave in such a manner out of their own volition. It is Satan who moves and prompts them to do so. I do not blame Satan, because he does not do anything without God's permission. I do not blame anyone, rather thank God in all situations because everything is done with permission by Him according to a plan for our good.

Also, the servants cannot be blamed for not attending the cattle, or for negligence or lack of vigilance in not noticing the movements of the neighbouring Sabeans. The servants were not in a position to do anything. Satan had permission from God and he incited the Sabeans to do what they did.

The Second Test

While the messenger was still speaking, another test by Satan took place, who had planned an accurate timetable for the sequence of tests so that they took place one after the other in such a manner that Job would not have time to recover from the previous test before he was to be hit by the following one, leading him to lose his senses. The next test was when a messenger came telling Job that God's fire came from Heaven and burnt the sheep and the servants.

At this stage perhaps Job was wondering: "God's fire? Is it possible that a fire comes down and burns the sheep? Was it not He who gave me the sheep and the servants? Would He send fire to burn them? "

Who sent the fire? With God's permission, Satan can perform acts in planets e.g he can send meteorites to cause fire in a certain way, in a certain size, and in a certain place to burn a certain area so as to burn a certain number of sheep and servants. The phrase "God's fire" was inspired by Satan to the messenger to give Job the impression that God was angry with him and an act of revenge against his evil, because the messenger actually saw it coming from heaven.

This test was actually very hard, because Job started doubting himself. Probably he started thinking: "My conscience is clear. Truly every human being is a sinner and lacking. But a fire from Heaven, O Lord? What have I done? Where did I go wrong?" It is possible that he thought: "There are people who commit such and such acts, You ignore them and burn my sheep only!" This test was particularly hard, because Satan began an attempt to create a rift between Job and God personally, because the previous test had caused a division between the Sabeans and Job, but in this test there were no Sabeans. It was an actual fire from Heaven which totally burnt the sheep and the servants.

The Third Test

"The Chaldeans formed three raiding parties and swept down on your camels and made off with them. They put the servants to the sword, and I am the only one who has escaped to tell you!"

At this stage, Job's mental ability to comprehend all these successive pieces of news of great catastrophes reached such an extent that he lost his sense of weighing things up. He could not digest this test because it was harder than the previous one. "They put the servants to the sword, and I am the only one who has escaped to tell you". In other words, had this messenger not been spared, the news would have reached Job much later, by which time he would have recovered from the shock. But, out of his evil, Satan spared one of the servants to enable him to speedily convey the news of this incident to Job in order to destroy him.

The Fourth Test

While he was still speaking, yet another messenger came and said, "Your sons and daughters were feasting and drinking wine at the oldest brother's house, when suddenly a mighty wind swept in from the desert and struck the four corners of the house. It collapsed on them and they are dead, and I am the only one who has escaped to tell you!"

With God's permission, Satan has the power to incite a mighty wind to sweep homes. Although winds have certain seasons, this particular wind was out of its season, because it was an act of Satan. The house was well-built and, because Job had the means, it was built on solid foundations, but what happened was an act of Satan - the house fell while Job's children were all feasting.

At this, Job got up and tore his robe and shaved his head. Then he fell to the ground in worship and said: "Naked I came from my mother's womb, and naked I will depart. The Lord gave and the Lord has taken away; may the name of the Lord be praised." In all this, Job did not sin by charging God with wrongdoing. (Job 1:7-22)

In olden times, tearing robes and shaving heads was a mourning tradition, similar to wearing black these days. When Job fell to the ground in worship and said: "Naked I came from my mother's womb, and naked I will depart....." he acknowledged the fact that when he came to this world, he did not own sheep, cattle, camels, servants or children. He was naked. Here we see Job's actual feelings. His response was actually heartfelt. It was the way he lived, and the way he reflected upon life. In spite of all the wealth he had, deep down he knew he was naked when he came to this world and would be naked when he left it. What he said was spontaneous and not read from books.

"As long as you walk on the path to the Kingdom and are approaching God's City, the strikes of trials will not leave you alone." - St. Maximous

JOB THANKS THE LORD FOR THE TEST

The Lord gave and the Lord has taken away; may the name of the Lord be praised. For example, let us say that you loaned me an amount of money and later on you asked me to return the money. Can I refuse to return it? Certainly not.

"The LORD gave and the LORD had taken away" In Job's comment about the Lord we see Job's great simplicity and submission. Would we react in the same manner under the same or similar situation? "In all this, Job did not sin by charging God with wrongdoing", which means that, even in his mind, Job was not resentful nor did he think that God was unfair. Regrettably, when it comes to the smallest problem, a person objects to God's will, saying, "Why does God do this to me? What did I do to deserve this?"

"I will endure ordeals so that I do not detach myself from the divine hope." - St. Isaac the Syrian

SUBMISSION THROUGH ORDEALS

"And he still maintains his integrity, though you incited Me against him to ruin him without any reason." This means that a person may be subjected to a test, and he tries to find a reason for it thinking: "Perhaps I sinned". Actually, anyone passing through a test ought to be humble enough to think: "This is because I sinned". There is a maxim in the book of "The Garden of Monks": "With each test which comes your way, say 'this is a result of my sin'".

The trials to which Job was subjected were not consequential to his sinning, because God testified that Job maintained his integrity. Even if we do not know the reason for our trials, we should not be saddened or resentful, rather thankful to God, because His will is for our own good.

Also, we are not to question the reason for the test: "But who are you, a human being, to talk back to God? "Shall what is formed say to the one who formed it, 'Why did you make me like...' "(Rom. 9:20). Watch the clay in the hands of the potter. He can shape it as he wishes: a flower pot, a water vessel or any other form he wishes. Can the clay ask the potter: why did you shape me this way?

"though you incited Me against him to ruin him without any reason." Here The Lord tells Satan:" you made Me subject him to harsh ordeals beyond endurance". As a matter of fact, these trials could have been beyond endurance to anyone other than Job, because trials are always for God's children and for those who are strong. St. Paul says: " ...but God is faithful; He will not let you be tempted beyond what you can bear."(1Cor.10:13)

As an illustration of the above verse, I give this example: when the goldsmith places the gold for purification in the crucible, he knows the temperature and time necessary for the process of purification. Gold needs time for purification more than any other mineral. The more the goldsmith increases the temperature, the purer the metal, because the increased temperature results in the burning of impurities, which either evaporate or turn into ashes with the heat. For example, the first to evaporate is lead, followed by tin and then copper. The gold is then purified and shines in the crucible.

In the same way God places a person under a test in order to burn the foreign elements of lust, deceit and all other sinful aspects. By the same token, when the goldsmith puts the gold in the crucible, he does not do so out of dislike. On the contrary, he does so to purify the gold from all impurities. The goldsmith does not increase the temperature to a degree which burns the gold. He increases the temperature to a degree just enough to burn the impurities. Similarly, God gives the test according to one's endurance. The test is a positive and not a negative act of God.

St. Paul says: "Endure hardship as discipline; God is treating you as his children. For what children are not disciplined by their father? If you are not disciplined – and everyone undergoes discipline – then you are not legitimate, not true sons and daughters at all. Moreover, we have all had human fathers who disciplined us and we respected them for it. How much more should we submit to the Father of spirits and live! They disciplined us for a little while as they thought best; but God disciplines us for our good, in order that we may share in His Holiness. No discipline seems pleasant at the time, but painful. Later on, however, it produces a harvest of righteousness and peace for those who have been trained by it." (Heb.12:7-11)

"'Skin for skin!' Satan replied. "A man will give all he has for his own life. But now stretch out Your Hand and strike his flesh and bones, and he will surely curse You to Your face." The Lord said to Satan, "Very well, then, he is in your hands; but you must spare his life." So Satan went out from the presence of the Lord and afflicted Job with painful sores from the soles of his feet to the crown of his head. Then Job took a piece of broken pottery and scraped himself with it as he sat among the ashes. His wife said to him, "Are you still maintaining your integrity? Curse God and die!" He replied, "You are talking like a foolish woman. Shall we accept good from God, and not trouble?" In all this, Job did not sin in what he said." (Job 2:4-10)

SATAN TRIES JOB IN HIS PERSON

"Skin for skin!" Satan replied. It was known that sacrificial animal offerings were skinned. "Skin for skin" meant that a person could offer a sacrifice as an atonement on his own behalf i.e. to redeem one's own skin. When Satan used the expression "skin for skin", he meant that all what Job had lost was a ransom for his own life. Here, it could be said to Satan: But earlier you said: "But now stretch out your hand and strike everything he has, and he will surely curse you to your face." And all this took place, he lost everything; he did not have even a single goat to provide him with milk to drink, yet Job never blasphemed as you claimed he would. Why then do you want to try him further?

Also, when Satan used this expression, he asked God that the test be carried out on the person of Job. In other words, on Job's skin and bones, and when God said: "Very well, then, he is in your hands....." He did not entirely surrender Job to Satan's hands, because He surrounded Job with His own hands, but in an invisible way. His grace filled Job's innermost heart. For this reason God allowed him to go through a test harsher than all the previous ones. "...... he is in your hands ...." Is it possible for a person to be in Satan's hands? This is a very harsh expression, which leads one to question: where is God's mercy? How would He leave us in Satan's hands?

Far be it from God. Truly a person may fall in the grip of Satan, but at the same time one is in God's stronghold. God ordered Satan: but you must spare his life. This means that tests are directed only to the body. Only God has authority over death; He is the only one who determines our lives. Jesus says: "And fear not them which kill the body, but are not able to kill the soul: but rather fear Him which is able to destroy both soul and body in hell." (Mt.10:28) At this Satan was happy when he left God's presence because he obtained permission to carry out his act, which reminds us of Jesus before He was to go through His final sufferings, when He said: "Simon, Simon, Satan has asked to sift all of you as wheat. But I have prayed for you, Simon, that your faith may not fail....." (Lk. 22:31-32)

Imagine Satan holding a sieve and the Apostles like wheat grains are tossed in every direction. What does a wheat grain weigh? How strong is it to resist the force of sifting? But Jesus interferes with His mighty protection: "But I have prayed for you, Simon, that your faith may not fail..."

So Satan went out from the presence of the Lord and afflicted Job with painful sores from the soles of his feet to the crown of his head. Can you imagine Job's pain? He was afflicted with painful sores from head to toe. One finds it painful enough if one finger is sore! Satan is very active in devising ways and means to hurt God's children. However, God transfers these sufferings into garlands of glory if they persevere in their faith. In His Second Coming, Jesus anticipates to find this faith: "However, when the Son of Man comes, will he find faith on the earth?" (Lk.18:8) St. Paul speaks to us about the spiritual weapons: "Above all, taking the shield of faith, wherewith ye shall be able to quench all the fiery darts of the evil one." (Eph.6:16)

Job's wife questioned his integrity in still clinging to his Lord. She insisted that he abandon his faith. Job rebuked her and told her that she was foolish because she accepted the good but was not prepared to accept trouble. He meant to say that, all that came from God was for one's good. In all this, Job did not sin by charging God with wrongdoing.

Sometimes, out of distress, one may sin through

uttering the wrong words, and at a later stage regrets what was said and prays to God for forgiveness. One may realize that whatever happened was trivial not warranting the manner in which one reacted. As for Job, in spite of all that had happened to him, never did he sin, not even by utterance. On the contrary he made a wonderful statement on which we should all reflect throughout our lives: "The Lord gave and the Lord has taken away; may the name of the Lord be praised."

"Being joyful during a test is evidence that you are leaving your ordeals behind." - St. Isaiah

"If you face an ordeal, do not search for its source or cause; but endure it without sorrow." - St. Mark

"Being prepared for pain for the sake of hope in God is truly great, which led St. Paul to describe it as a "gift", when he said: 'You are gifted for Jesus' sake, not only to believe in Him, but also to suffer for His sake'." - St. Isaac the Syrian

Chapter 6

"And lead us not into temptation, but deliver us from evil"

"Watch and pray so that you will not fall into temptation. The spirit is willing, but the flesh is weak."

- Mt: 26:41

Some think of the above section of the LORD's prayer as two sentences: that is "And lead us not into temptation" and "but deliver us from evil". However, in my mind I think of it as one sentence, that is, "And lead us not into temptation, but deliver us from evil", because the one who leads us into temptation is Satan (also called the tempter or the accuser). This was evidenced when Jesus came out of the River Jordan and was filled with the Holy Spirit; "Jesus was led by the Spirit into the wilderness to be tempted by the devil."(Mt. 4:1). Also, in the Book of Revelation it is stated: "For the accuser of our brothers and sisters, who accuses them before our God day and night, has been hurled down."(Rev. 12:10). In Job's example, it was Satan who put him to the test.

When we pray, why do we say "And lead us not into temptation ", even though we are tested by Satan? Because the tempter does not lead us into temptation unless he is permitted by God. The tempter does not have a free hand to test the person as he wishes.

It was Jesus who taught us to pray: and lead us not into temptation. He knew our weakness. He knew that because of our weakness, we might not be able to endure the test. Some tests are beyond a person's endurance, but through God's grace one is given the strength, the perseverance and the blessing to endure: "Watch and pray so that you will not fall into temptation. The spirit is willing, but the flesh is weak." (Mt. 26:41)

One may argue: If you are strong, with a solid faith, and totally reliant on our LORD's Grace, you should not say "Do not lead us into temptation ", rather say:

"I will go through the temptation and I do not care about anything ". This is wrong. It reflects arrogance, and once grace forsakes you, you cannot bear the test not even for a single day, regardless of how saintly you are.

"And lead us not into temptation, but deliver us from evil". Also, one may argue: there is no such one called Satan, nor is there a so-called evil one. Satan may even convince a person to this effect saying: Do not believe that there is such a thing called Satan because your thoughts are of your own making. However, Satan actually exists. He is the tempter; he is so intelligent as to convince a person that there is no such a thing as Satan. If Satan tempted the Saviour Himself, how is it that we cannot also fall into his temptations? Saints Antonious and Abu Maqar actually saw Satan.

"But deliver us from the evil" Not all sins committed by a person are from Satan, because some sins and tests are acts committed by the person himself and Satan has nothing to do with them. For example: If at one stage Satan led you to a particular sin, then left you alone, and regrettably, later on you kept repeating this sin several times until it becomes a habit, in this case your falling into sin becomes out of your own will.

REASONS FOR OUR BEING LED INTO TEMPTATION

1 - Because of Sin:

In many instances, illness is a result of sin. This is evidenced in the case of the invalid of Bethesda when the LORD told him: "See, you are well again. Stop sinning or something worse may happen to you." (Jn. 5:14). In this instance, the LORD demonstrated to the Bethesda's invalid that he was the cause of the illness, by warning him that if he sinned again something worse might happen to him. Based on this statement it may be said that if the Lord's hand is withheld from healing (unwilling to heal) this is due to non-repentance from sin: " Behold, the Lord's hand is not shortened, But your iniquities have separated between you and your God" (Isa.59:1), meaning that sin is the basic reason for God to withhold His hand from healing.

One's evil desire or lust is one of the factors of our being led into temptation. "But each person is tempted when they are dragged away by their own evil desire and enticed. Then, after desire has conceived, it gives birth to sin; and sin, when it is full-grown, gives birth to death." (James 13-15).

My beloved brethren, do not stray by thinking that God has anything to do with the tests resulting from evil desire, because every good gift comes from Him, but anything else which is not good ends up in death. These types of tests are not from God and He does not lead a person to them. It is a person's choice to be led to these tests, because " ....they are dragged away by their own evil desire and enticed."

2 - For Discipline and Reform

" The purpose of tests is either discipline because of the sins which we committed in the past, so that they may be erased, or reform because of our existing laxity in our spiritual life, or to prevent us from committing future sins." - St. Maximous.

The Lord disciplines the arrogant by allowing the test in order to humble them. This is demonstrated in an anecdote from the life of St. Pakhomious; One of his disciples asked him every now and then to pray for him. St. Pakhomious asked him, "What do you wish me to pray for?" The disciple monk replied, "You pray that I die a martyr." The saint responded, "No". However, the disciple persisted and the saint kept saying that it was not his time yet. However, the monk over-estimated himself, was not obedient neither was he humble and he continued in his persistence.

One day, St. Pakhomious' disciples were chopping wood in a remote place. They lived in the location during that period. St. Pakhomious went to the monk who had the desire for martyrdom and asked him to take some food and wine and visit his brethren who were carrying out a hard task.

The monk took the provisions and went to see his brethren. On the way, he was met by heathens who worshiped the sun and idols. They took the provisions from him, tied his hands and ordered him to join them to offer sacrifice and incense to their idols because they were celebrating one of their heathen feasts and they also ordered him to share with them their banquet, which was also an offering to their idols. They threatened him with the sword that if he refused, they would kill him. The monk weakened, and out of fear, participated in their rituals.

The monk returned crying to St. Pakhomious, who

told him, "You, poor man. More than once you asked me to pray for you because it was your wish to die a martyr and I used to tell you not to ask for something beyond your ability. When you got what you desired, you coward. Now, go back to your cell, remain in it for a year, do not eat anything other than bread and salt and weep in repentance for your sin."

God shields the humble, but those who are proud of themselves and boastful of their abilities, are forsaken by Grace and become exposed to trials. When standing before God, one must stand admitting one's weakness and pray humbly: for the sake of Your Holy Name and for the sake of Your saints, lead us not into temptation. St. Isaac says: "He who is boastful of his celibacy, falls into the sin of adultery. He who is boastful of his wisdom, education and knowledge, falls into the sin of blasphemy."

3 – To Enrich the Faith

This was evidenced in the incident when the LORD urged the disciples to go into the boat to face the tempest and this was a test of their faith. The Lord Jesus knew that the disciples' faith was weak. It was necessary to elevate them to a higher level of faith. This could not be realized unless they were subjected to the test.

In a test, the Lord is revealed to you through His power and authority when he transforms the darkness into light. From the depth of the test our faith in God is elevated.

4 – For Glory and Reward

The Lord allows the saints to go through tests so that they may be blessed and so that their patience and faith is seen by others. "Blessed is the one who perseveres under trial because, having stood the test, that person will receive the crown of life that the Lord has promised to those who love him." (James 1:12)

An example was a saint called Abba Bemwah. This saint was ill for 12 years. Even though he was a great saint, the Lord allowed his illness to crush him for 12 years, until he reached the state of perfection.

GOD'S WORD IS THE SUPPORT IN TRIALS

When a believer's faith is tested either by hardships, illness or persecution, he seeks comfort in reading the Bible. Through the Bible, the Lord speaks to the person in trouble. He gives solace to the sorrowful soul. Comfort and joy replace anxiety and sorrow.

I ought to accept hardships and trials with joy, because they bring me closer to God. How can we be happy in hardships and trials, although in most cases these are sorrows, illnesses or persecutions? In the Acts of the Apostles, it was mentioned that: "The apostles left the Sanhedrin, rejoicing because they had been counted worthy of suffering disgrace for the....." (Acts 5:41). One may ask: how could they rejoice even though every now and then they were scourged? Because they had been counted worthy of suffering disgrace for the sake of His name. Saints Paul and Silas were scourged and thrown into prison and their feet chained, nevertheless they joyfully praised God through the night.

Some people may face problems which go on for months or even a lifetime without finding solutions for them. This can be attributed to the absence of God's Word, which nurtures the soul and enlightens the mind: "Your word is a lamp for my feet, and a light on my path." (Ps.119:105)

Sometimes we find homes full of problems to such an extent that the home itself is on the verge of collapse. The first impression is that it may be attributed to financial difficulties. Then we find that they have an affluent living. Could it be because of children's failure in studies? No. They are all successful. Eventually, we find the vital reason is the absence of God from the home. God's word is the support to the body and the light to the mind: "When anxiety was great within me, Your consolation brought me joy." (Ps.94:19) There is no remedy for the human race unless it is nurtured with God's Word.

May God bless all of us to be steadfast in ordeals and give us guidance in trials so that we are triumphant through the power of the cross of our Lord Jesus Christ

www.ingramcontent.com/pod-product-compliance
Lightning Source LLC
Chambersburg PA
CBHW021912040426
42447CB00007B/825